Giving God Your Whole Heart

The Path to True Fulfillment

Bridget A. Thomas

All scripture quotations are taken from the Holy Bible, New International Version, unless stated otherwise.

THE HOLY BIBLE, NEW INTERNATIONAL VERSION®, NIV® Copyright © 1973, 1978, 1984, 2011 by Biblica, Inc.® Used by permission. All rights reserved worldwide. "New International Version" and "NIV" are registered trademarks of Biblica, Inc.®

The King James Version (KJV) is public domain in the United States.

Visit the author's website at bridgetathomas.com.

Cover design and artistic design by Stacey Witkowski, StaceyWitkowski.com.

Edited by Brittany Clarke, brittclarke.com.

Disclaimer: The author of this book is not a licensed counselor. This book is not intended as a guide to diagnose any medical or psychological issues. If expert assistance is needed, please seek help from a healthcare provider or licensed counselor. This work is sold with the understanding that neither the author nor the publisher are held responsible for a perceived negative outcome as a result of the contents of this book.

ISBN-13: 978-1-7322020-5-4
ISBN-10: 1-7322020-5-2

Dedication

This book is dedicated to my husband, Mickey, whose love, support, and prayers have kept me going.

I also dedicate this book to my parents, who have been faithfully cheering me on throughout this journey.

Chapter 1 – Making a Decision

Some birthdays hit us harder than others. On one particular birthday for me, I knew I had to make some changes. I looked back over my life and wondered where the time had gone. It seemed to have gone by in a flash. Did I always make the best choices? Could I look back on my life and be content with where I was? I had many blessings in my life to be thankful for. I had a loving husband, a supportive family, a great job, and a beautiful home. However, not everything was the way I wanted it to be. I felt as though I was still missing out on so much. I knew my relationships could be better. I knew I had a lot of work on the inside to accomplish. I knew I wanted to be stronger in many areas of my life. But what I ultimately knew most of all was that I needed to make one particular decision to see true change in my life.

I needed to give God my whole heart. I needed to go all in. Even though I was committed to the Lord, I still allowed many things to come between Him and myself. I had a tendency to stack bricks around my heart, to build a wall between myself and anything else that made me uneasy at times. Unfortunately, this included God. I wanted my life to be comfortable, and I knew God wanted me to make changes which would disrupt this illusion of comfort. When you build a wall around your heart, though, it doesn't just keep out the negative feelings, it also keeps out the positive ones. So I finally understood in order to find joy in my life, I had to make some alterations in my life. I had to take down the bricks, one-by-one. Deep within my core I knew that once I got this area of my life on track, I would see positive changes in all other areas.

In order to get myself on track, I started asking myself two questions:

- Am I giving God my whole heart?
- Who do I want to be?

These two questions helped me to make better decisions. They helped me to be more open with God. They helped me to be more loving to the people I encountered. They helped me to overcome obstacles that got in my way. I believe they can do the same for you. Once you begin to give God your whole heart, you will see radical change in your life. You will have more joy and peace in your life. Once we get our relationship with God on solid ground, we can rest assured that everything else in our lives will improve. God has to be the foundation in our lives. Then we can build a strong home on top of the foundation.

I am convinced that our world would have much fewer problems if people gave God their whole hearts. We would see more love and less hate. We would see more people being fed and fewer people going hungry. We would see more people being considerate of one another instead of acting selfishly. We would all overcome more mountains in our lives, instead of allowing those mountains to defeat us. We would see a drastically different world than the one we see now when we turn on the news or step out our front door.

While we might not be able to force the rest of the world to give God their whole hearts, we can at least start with our own hearts. So what about you? Are you ready to see positive changes in your life? Are you ready to have more joy and peace? Are you ready to be more victorious in every area of your life? Are you ready to give God your whole heart?

God Wants Us

Love. It is a constant, universal desire. We all want someone to love us and to demonstrate their love for us by making us feel accepted, appreciated, and understood. Yet we cannot rely on other people to love us every single second of every single day. Other people will fail in this area from time to time. No one is perfect, and no one can love perfectly. No one, except God. God can love us all the time. And He does. He always accepts us, always appreciates us, and always understands us. God loves us with an unconditional and everlasting love. Even when we make mistakes, even when we mess up, even when we are at our worst, God still loves us.

I believe the reason why many people do not give God their whole heart is because they haven't fully accepted His love for them. The Bible says, "We love because He first loved us" (1 John 4:19). Loving God comes more easily when we fully embrace His love for us. As we grow in our understanding of how much God truly loves us, it causes us to want to love Him in return with all our heart, mind, and soul, as we are commanded to do (Matthew 22:37).

It also makes us want to hand Him the reins and allow Him to have control of our lives. We see that He can handle everything much better than we have without Him. When we try to do things in life by our own strength, we fall short. We make plans, we try to accomplish things, we set goals, but undertaken by our own feeble efforts, those things often crumble. Once we allow God to be King of our lives, we will see miracles happen. Because we have the Lord guiding our lives and directing our steps, we will build stronger relationships, see our goals accomplished, have peace in our hearts, find purpose, and ultimately finally find true fulfillment.

God wants to be part of our lives. God wants to be our friend. God wants to be our companion. God wants to have an intimate relationship with each and every one of us. God wants us to seek Him. God wants to help us with decisions in our lives. God wants to steer us down life's path. God wants to help us overcome obstacles. God wants to bless us. The bottom line is that God wants us.

How beautiful is that? The King of kings and Lord of lords wants us. I don't know about you, but this alone makes me want to love God with all my heart, mind, and soul. It makes me want to love God every moment of every day. It makes me want to seek God and get to know Him better. It makes me want to spread His love to those around me and be a better person. It makes me want to do His will. It makes me want to be a shining light in this dark world. It makes me want to give God my whole heart.

When I was growing up, we would attend church off and on. I remember going to a Methodist church for the longest stretch. We also went to churches of other denominations here and there, such as a Lutheran church. However, when we visited my grandmother, who lived in another state, it was obvious to me that she had something I didn't. She had Jesus. While I knew of Jesus, my grandmother really seemed to have a genuine relationship with Him. She talked about Him a lot. He brought her happiness.

When I was twelve, I wanted in on it. I decided I wanted to have this relationship as well. I was initially excited about this new path. I tried to read my Bible, like I saw my grandmother doing. Even many adults have a hard time making it very far into the Bible, though, so imagine a twelve-year-old doing this. Sadly, I wound up laying my Bible aside.

Most days, I was a thousand miles away from my grandmother. I didn't really know how to be a Christian, what I was supposed to do, or how I was supposed to live. Therefore, I just did the things I'd always done. I didn't give God my whole heart because I didn't know how. And this meant I didn't live my life for God either. I just did the things the world did, and I did all the things my friends did, because that was what appeared normal to me. When I was a teenager, we began attending a non-denominational church. I really loved the services, the music, and the sermons. But unfortunately I still didn't know what I was to do when I walked out the door of the church. My life continued like this for many years.

Yet all the while I knew I was missing something. I felt empty at times. Slowly, I began to seek change. I wanted more out of life. I knew I needed something and I turned to God. But it wasn't like I snapped my fingers and then all of a sudden everything was perfect. It took time. Learning how to give God my whole heart was a process, and that process is still ongoing. I'm still not perfect. This is a life long journey we are all on of drawing closer to God every day of our earthly lives.

I tell you all of that to say that I have lived with God and I have lived without God. And I can tell you that living with God has brought me much more happiness and peace than living without God ever did. I do not want to go back to the person I was without Him. Just thinking about those days makes me feel sad and depleted. Now I feel as though I have been made new... because I have! When we give our lives to God, we become a new creature (2 Corinthians 5:17). He changes us from the inside out, if we allow Him to. And why wouldn't we want that when what He has to offer is so much more fulfilling than anything we can get on our own?

The Prodigal Son

It doesn't matter where you are in life or how your relationship with God looks. You can make a change right now. You might be familiar with the story of the lost son, or who many people refer to as the prodigal son, found in Luke 15:11-32. Let's look at it together:

> *Jesus continued: "There was a man who had two sons. The younger one said to his father, 'Father, give me my share of the estate.' So he divided his property between them.*

> *"Not long after that, the younger son got together all he had, set off for a distant country and there squandered his wealth in wild living. After he had spent everything, there was a severe famine in that whole country, and he began to be in need. So he went and hired himself out to a citizen of that country, who sent him to his fields to feed pigs. He longed to fill his stomach with the pods that the pigs were eating, but no one gave him anything.*

"When he came to his senses, he said, 'How many of my father's hired servants have food to spare, and here I am starving to death! I will set out and go back to my father and say to him: Father, I have sinned against heaven and against you. I am no longer worthy to be called your son; make me like one of your hired servants.' So he got up and went to his father.

"But while he was still a long way off, his father saw him and was filled with compassion for him; he ran to his son, threw his arms around him and kissed him.

"The son said to him, 'Father, I have sinned against heaven and against you. I am no longer worthy to be called your son.'

"But the father said to his servants, 'Quick! Bring the best robe and put it on him. Put a ring on his finger and sandals on his feet. Bring the fattened calf and kill it. Let's have a feast and celebrate. For this son of mine was dead and is alive again; he was lost and is found.' So they began to celebrate.

"Meanwhile, the older son was in the field. When he came near the house, he heard music and dancing. So he called one of the servants and asked him what was going on. 'Your brother has come,' he replied, 'and your father has killed the fattened calf because he has him back safe and sound.'

"The older brother became angry and refused to go in. So his father went out and pleaded with him. But he answered his father, 'Look! All these years I've been slaving for you and never disobeyed your orders. Yet you never gave me even a young goat so I could celebrate with my friends. But when this son of yours who has squandered your property with prostitutes comes home, you kill the fattened calf for him!'

"'My son,' the father said, 'you are always with me, and everything I have is yours. But we had to celebrate and be glad, because this brother of yours was dead and is alive again; he was lost and is found.'"

The father in this parable was so thrilled to see his younger son had returned home. It didn't matter to him what he'd done while he was gone; he only cared that he was back.

The son's heart had been turned toward money, food, and wild living. Then miraculously his heart was restored and he returned to his true identity. The father blessed him with the best of everything when he came back home. This is how it is with God and His children. No matter where we are or what we've done, He is willing to take us back into His arms. He loves us beyond measure. God wants to bless us with the best of everything. But we have to make the decision to bring our whole heart back to Him first.

Reflection

What does giving God your whole heart mean to you?

_____

_____

_____

_____

_____

Do you want to have a stronger relationship with God?

_____

_____

_____

_____

_____

Are there any changes in your life that you can make in order to draw closer to the Lord?

_____

_____

_____

_____

_____

Chapter 2 – A Lamp for My Feet

My husband and I love visiting the Smoky Mountains. It is such a peaceful and serene area. While we are there, we spend much of our time out in nature. We especially love a certain place within the Great Smoky Mountains National Park called Cades Cove. This is an eleven-mile loop where you can drive your car around and see a lot of wildlife. We often see bears, deer, turkey, squirrels, birds, and sometimes even coyotes. Cades Cove also has old cabins and churches, hiking trails, beautiful waterfalls, horse stables for rides through the park, and camping sites. It is truly a delight to go there. We love Cades Cove so much that we actually set an alarm clock most mornings so we can get there when they open. We visit it at least once a day while we're in the mountains and spend several hours riding around and looking for wildlife. It's amazing how spending time in nature can rejuvenate your soul. Getting outdoors can be so therapeutic.

However, the last trip we went on, after several days of being there, I realized that I felt off. Even though we were spending hours breathing in fresh air, I still didn't feel refreshed. It was almost like I was in a fog. I would see all the gorgeous scenery, but I wasn't quite absorbing it all. I wondered why I wasn't fully enjoying my vacation, until I realized that we had been so busy while on our trip that I hadn't read my Bible in several days. When we got back to our cabin that day, I pulled my Bible out of my suitcase to read. Even just holding the book in my hands, I immediately felt so much better. It was like my soul let out a soft sigh of contentment.

One of the most important things to remember when giving God our whole heart, is that reading the Bible is of utmost importance. It is essential to our well-being and our growth. It provides our souls with nourishment, just as food does for our bodies. This one habit can dramatically transform our day.

For many years I didn't make reading my Bible a priority. I thought that reading Christian non-fiction books and listening to sermons was good enough. I was wrong, though, and everything in my life was proof. I made bad choices, and I didn't have any true peace. One day I tried to make reading my Bible a priority, but sadly, I still didn't give it my all. I would hurry through a chapter and not necessarily retain what I read. I knew that I was still missing out on so much in my walk with the Lord. I had a longing to know Him better. I had a thirst for Him. Deep down I knew that digging deeper and immersing myself in my Bible reading would be a big key to seeing changes in my life.

At one point, I felt God prompt me to start my day off right by reading my Bible first thing in the morning. This would mean getting up earlier to spend some time with Him before I did anything else. I'll be honest, I really did not want to get up earlier. I already got up very early for work. And at this particular season of my life, I was tired a lot and had in fact been looking for ways to get extra sleep. But the funny thing was, when I tried to sleep in later, I would still wake up early. I knew this was God, gently pushing me. So, I finally turned back the time on my alarm clock. I spent some time first thing in the morning focused on my Bible, trying to eliminate other distractions. Let me just tell you that I actually felt more refreshed, not tired! How remarkable is that? Also, since my brain was fresh after a good night's rest, I soaked in so much more of what God was trying to teach me.

Why Is Reading the Bible Important?

Reading our Bibles is an essential component of our Christian walk. Now that it is a part of my daily life, I can definitely see how I have changed for the better because of it. Here are just a few reasons why reading the Bible is crucial for giving God your whole heart.

The Bible is one way we get to know God. When we became Christians, we entered into a relationship with the Lord. In our earthly relationships with other people, we get to know them by spending time with them. When two young people are dating, for instance, it is understood that they are spending time together. Two people wouldn't say they are dating and then never actually get together. They want to meet up at a restaurant or a park so they can have some face-to-face time. They want to learn about each other, about each other's likes and dislikes, quirks, character, and childhood. They are so interested in each other that both want to know everything there is to know about the other! Reading our Bibles is similar in that it is a prime way of spending time with God. As we read, we learn about His character. We see His history and the different things He's done in the past. We get to know what's important to Him. And most of all, we discover how loving He is.

The Bible also helps us in battle. The truth is that we live in a fallen world, and as Christians we are going to see adversity. Much of it, I believe, comes from Satan. He is our enemy whose desire is to bring us down, which means we have to be prepared. When a young person joins the army, he goes through training. In the beginning he has to go through boot camp, which gets him into shape quickly. Even when boot camp is over, he doesn't cease to keep his body fit. He doesn't stop his target practice. He has to stay sharp and ready in case of battle. The same is true for Christians. We have to be ready every single day. Our enemy doesn't stop. He doesn't take a nap, and he doesn't declare peace. So we too need to be on guard at all times, and the Bible is our weapon.

Hebrews 4:12 says, "For the word of God is alive and active. Sharper than any double-edged sword, it penetrates even to dividing soul and spirit, joints and marrow; it judges the thoughts and attitudes of the heart." This verse shows us how powerful the Bible is. When we are faced with any adversity, we can use Bible verses as our armor. This is precisely what Jesus did when the devil tried to tempt Him, in Luke 4:1-13:

> *Jesus, full of the Holy Spirit, left the Jordan and was led by the Spirit into the wilderness, where for*

forty days he was tempted by the devil. He ate nothing during those days, and at the end of them he was hungry.

The devil said to him, "If you are the Son of God, tell this stone to become bread."

Jesus answered, "It is written: 'Man shall not live on bread alone.'"

The devil led him up to a high place and showed him in an instant all the kingdoms of the world. And he said to him, "I will give you all their authority and splendor; it has been given to me, and I can give it to anyone I want to. If you worship me, it will all be yours."

Jesus answered, "It is written: 'Worship the Lord your God and serve him only.'"

The devil led him to Jerusalem and had him stand on the highest point of the temple. "If you are the Son of God," he said, "throw yourself down from here. For it is written:

"'He will command his angels concerning you to guard you carefully; they will lift you up in their hands, so that you will not strike your foot against a stone.'"

Jesus answered, "It is said: 'Do not put the Lord your God to the test.'"

When the devil had finished all this tempting, he left him until an opportune time.

Jesus always came back at the enemy with a verse from Scripture, and we can do the same. When we are faced with something difficult, we can use Scripture as our defense. Here are some practical examples:

- If you feel you are being attacked or wronged by someone, you can use Isaiah 54:17, which says, "No weapon forged against you will prevail."

- If you are facing an illness, you can remember Mark 10:52, where Jesus tells a blind man, named Bartimaeus, "Your faith has healed you."

- If you are feeling brokenhearted, consider Psalm 147:3, which says, "He heals the brokenhearted and binds up their wounds."

These are just a few illustrations of how you can use Scripture for difficulties in your life. Whatever it is you are up against, you can surely find a verse to help you through your struggle. Your Bible might have a concordance in the back that you can use to look for verses related to a particular topic. Or you can also find verses on the internet, which is the route I take most often. Simply search for something like, "Bible verses about _____." Fill in the blank with whatever your current issue is. Many times you will find a comprehensive list of verses pertaining to that topic.

Finally, the Bible helps us make decisions in life. Psalm 119:105 says, "Your word is a lamp for my feet, a light on my path." We make thousands of decisions every day. Some are seemingly unimportant, such as which outfit to wear. Others, though, are significant, and these bigger decisions may leave us unsure of the best route to take. The world bases its decisions off of wants, feelings, and what everyone else is doing. But, as Christians, we are not of this world and we shouldn't make our decisions in the same way the world does. The Bible gives us clear guidelines on how we are to live, what we are to do with our money, how we are to treat others, and so on.

Come Close to God

Reading the Bible brings us closer to God. It says in James 4:8, "Come near to God and he will come near to you." If you are longing for a deeper relationship with the Lord but haven't been dedicated to reading Scripture, you can start today. Set aside some time in your schedule to read your Bible. You don't need a lot of time. You can start with five minutes, if that is all you have. Hopefully down the road you will be able to increase your time with Him each day. The first step is just showing up. As you continually show up day after day, you will notice a difference in your mood, your inner thoughts, and your life. Psalm 19:7 tells us, "The law of the Lord is perfect, refreshing the soul. The statutes of the Lord are trustworthy, making wise the simple." The Word of God is alive and it is so astounding how it can breathe life into each one of us.

I can tell you from my own experience that making Scripture reading a part of my mornings has truly transformed my life. When I take time to read my Bible, it starts my day off on the right foot. I have an inner peace and calmness, even when troubles arise. And on days when

I do not read my Bible, I feel flustered. Reading the Bible is a privilege and a treasure. God left us a tool that we can refer to again and again. Personally, I am very thankful that the Lord has given us this precious gift.

As it says in 2 Peter 1:2, "Grace and peace be yours in abundance through the knowledge of God and of Jesus our Lord."

Reflection

Is reading your Bible a priority in your daily routine?

_____

_____

_____

_____

_____

If the answer is yes, how has this habit made a difference in your life? If the answer is no, what can you do to carve out some time in your day to read your Bible?

_____

_____

_____

_____

_____

Think of something you are struggling with in your life right now. Now take a few minutes to look up Bible verses that you might use when facing this battle.

_____

_____

_____

Chapter 3 – Pray Continually

Have you ever thought about what an honor it is for us to be able to speak to the King of kings anytime we want to? Not only that, but have you considered how He is always there? He will never say He is busy. He will never ignore us. He will never tell us to come back another time. His door is always open. He is just waiting for us to come to Him.

In the book of Exodus, we read about the tabernacle, which is where the Israelites would go to offer sacrifices to God and to worship Him. Within the tabernacle was the Ark of the Covenant, the place where God's Spirit resided. There was a curtain that separated the Ark of the Covenant from the rest of the tabernacle. The high priest was the only one who could go beyond the curtain, and that was only once a year, on the Day of Atonement. In Matthew 27:51, when referring to the moment when Jesus died, the Bible says, "At that moment the curtain of the temple was torn in two from top to bottom. The earth shook, the rocks split." The curtain's being torn in two is significant. Jesus' death on the cross meant that we could now meet with the Lord. We have access to the Most High God, anytime and anywhere, through prayer. What a privilege we have!

Prayer is the root of our faith. Our walk with the Lord often begins with a prayer. Our daily lives should be covered with prayer. And prayer is often where much of our inner work is accomplished. If we want to give God our whole heart, we have to take time to meet Him in prayer.

Prayer is so very powerful. A couple of years ago I spoke to a loved one on the phone who was in the hospital. She was scared, depressed, anxious, lonely, and confused. It hurt my heart that I could not be with her in person since she lived in another state. So I posted on social media asking my friends for their help with an unspoken prayer request. The next morning I called this loved one again and she sounded completely different. She was upbeat, positive, and optimistic. Prayer transformed this situation. I almost couldn't believe it myself, seeing this miracle occur. But I know how awesome God is!

Sometimes when we, or our loved ones, are facing something difficult, we feel helpless. However, the truth is that we are not helpless at all. We have prayer, and prayer is the most valuable asset in the midst of a battle.

There are times when we might not know what words we should speak in our prayers. Perhaps we are in too much pain or are too confused about what we are facing to form a coherent string of thoughts. Or, as was the case in the story I just shared above, sometimes we don't know exactly what we are praying for because we don't have all the details. That's okay! Because God knows it all! He knows exactly what we need. He knows better than we do how we are feeling and what we are facing. Romans 8:26-27 says,

> *The Spirit helps us in our weakness. We do not know what we ought to pray for, but the Spirit himself intercedes for us through wordless groans. And he who searches our hearts knows the mind of the Spirit, because the Spirit intercedes for God's people in accordance with the will of God.*

How astounding it is to know that the Holy Spirit intercedes for us, in harmony with God's will. I am just speechless when I think about that. When you can't even seem to think of the proper words to pray, you can rest assured the Holy Spirit has your back.

Trials

When we are facing trials in our lives, prayer is always a good place to start. Whatever difficulty you are facing, God can handle it. Bring your worries to Him. Ask Him to help you with whatever obstacle is in front of you. He can move mountains. He can perform miracles. He can break any chain that is holding you back. He will make a way. Sometimes it might seem like the road in front of you goes nowhere. You were driving along at a good pace, but then you came to a halt because the road ahead was under construction. Maybe you've been siting there waiting with the car in park for a while and you're losing hope. Don't give up. God is paving the way. But it all has to start with your prayer.

Now, I know some of you might be thinking of times when your prayers weren't answered. However, it is important to note that just because God didn't work things out exactly the way you wanted doesn't mean He wasn't listening. God knows what is best for us, and we ultimately have to trust Him to work things out according to His will.

Another significant point I want to make is that often times when we go through trials, God will use them to change us. He does not necessarily create all the trials in our lives. However, He can still use them to build our character, to mold us into our best selves, and to strengthen us in our walk. James 1:2-4 says, "Consider it pure joy, my brothers and sisters, whenever you face trials of many kinds, because you know that the testing of your faith produces perseverance. Let perseverance finish its work so that you may be mature and complete, not lacking anything."

I have a bad habit. When something uncomfortable occurs in my life, I am quick to ask God to take it away. I am trying to change my perspective, though, and remember that God will use trials to strengthen us, prepare us for the future, and ultimately mold us to be more like Jesus.

Let's take a look at a biblical example of how trials can reform us. One of the most beloved characters in the Bible is King David, who was the finest king that Israel ever had. David faced many trials in his life, before and after becoming king. He is most remembered for killing the giant named Goliath, but he could not have done this if he had not first endured some prior trials in his life which helped mold him. Israel's troops were terrified of Goliath. For forty days he taunted them, but no one took a stand against him. Finally, one day when David came to deliver food to his brothers, he was the one to take a stand.

Let's back up a little bit. In 1 Samuel chapter 16, when we first learn that David was to one day be king, we also discover that he tended his father's sheep. This might sound like an easy task. It might be perceived that this job wouldn't involve much conflict or trouble. However, let's take a look at 1 Samuel 17:34-37, where David speaks to Saul, king of Israel at the time, about how his modest job had prepared him to take on Goliath:

> *But David said to Saul, "Your servant has been keeping his father's sheep. When a lion or a bear came and carried off a sheep from the flock, I went after it, struck it and rescued the sheep from its mouth. When it turned on me, I seized it by its hair, struck it and killed it. Your servant has killed both the lion and the bear; this uncircumcised Philistine will be like one of them, because he has defied the armies of the living God. The Lord who rescued me from the paw of the lion and the paw of the bear will rescue me from the hand of this Philistine."*

Because of his past trials, David knew the power of the Lord, and thus faced Goliath and defeated the nine-foot-tall giant with a slingshot and a rock. If David had never faced a lion or a bear when he was tending his father's sheep, would we have ever read about a time when he defeated Goliath?

This story is such an important reminder to me that we need to have a different perspective when trials come our way. I believe it is okay to still pray about them. The power of prayer can help us defeat the trials in our lives. However, I think it would also do us good to remember how God is using those trials to shape us and strengthen us.

Giving Thanks

I don't think I have to take a survey to assert that most prayers consist of requests. I know for me personally this is true. I often ask God to protect my loved ones, to help me with tasks on my plate, to move a mountain I am facing, and so on. While I believe it is okay to ask God for His help, I noticed that in my own prayer life, I was spending too much time asking and not enough time praising. I believe that in our prayers, it is essential to thank God for things, and to praise Him for how overwhelmingly wonderful He is.

God helps us so much each and every day. I am convinced that there are so many things He does to protect us in our daily lives that we don't even realize. For example, when I am delayed in getting out the door, is it really God who sets me back in order to avoid an accident? It is very possible. And I have to wonder how many times things like this happen in our day that we are ignorant of. One early morning when I was driving to work, God helped me dodge a metal trash can that was on the interstate and nearly impossible to see in the dark. I routinely drove to work in the dark, so this experience caused me to wonder how many instances there had been when God protected me from unseen objects on the road. It makes me want to praise Him for His goodness and for His divine protection!

A couple of years ago, I learned a lesson in giving thanks when my husband and I were planning one of our trips to the mountains. I get a little overwhelmed when I'm packing because I have too many decisions to make and think about, so I use a list to keep myself organized. It helps a lot, as long as I follow the list, and as long as I don't leave anything off the list. As I was packing on this particular day, my thoughts were getting a bit frazzled. I began to worry about our safety on the trip. It was a long drive, and I fretted over the possibility of getting in an accident. When I let my thoughts go like a runaway train, I start to feel anxious and edgy. This is where I was headed on this day. As I continued to pack, I felt God remind me to pack my husband's cholesterol medicine. I had forgotten it on my list, and I was so thankful for the reminder.

This struck me in an interesting way. While I was in the midst of feeling worried and nervous about our safety on the trip, God showed me how much He truly looks out for us. How could I doubt His divine protection when He had just helped me remember to pack something that was not on my list? This was an eye-opening experience for me, because it allowed me to see first-hand how much God does look out for us, even in seemingly small things. It made me want to shower God with praise and thanksgiving.

Journaling

If you want to improve your prayer life, you might want to consider using a prayer journal. This is a perfect way to keep track of prayers. Write down the different struggles you're dealing with and ask for God's help and guidance with each one. Also, when you tell someone else that you will pray for them, write it down in your prayer journal as well. A prayer journal can also be used to give thanks to the Lord. When you see that a prayer has been answered, write it down and thank God for it. When you see a blessing the Lord has given you, jot it down in your prayer journal and give thanks.

In essence, your prayer journal might consist of things you have asked for as well as things you are grateful for. In time you will be able to look back at all the prayers God has answered. When we see the evidence of His love in this way, it will evoke in us a desire to praise Him more and more. It will help us to learn to trust Him more. And it will show us just how much He really does look out for us, in big and small matters.

When giving God your whole heart, it is important to remember the strong communication line we have with Him in prayer. Whatever you might be going through today, remember how amazing God is and hand it over to Him! Prayer is such a mighty treasure we Christians have. We can pray anytime and anywhere, trusting that God is always there. He loves His children and wants to be there for them. Just as any loving parent wants to help their children, God wants to help us. Take a step to the throne and lay your worries at His feet.

Reflection

Take a moment to think about your prayer life. Are you satisfied with it? If not, how can you improve it?

_____

_____

_____

_____

_____

What trials are you facing in your life right now? Do you think there is anything God is trying to teach you or change in you in the midst of this trial?

_____

_____

_____

_____

Do you make a habit of thanking God for the answered prayers and blessings in your life? If not, how can you improve in this area?

_____

Chapter 4 – Seeking and Listening

Are there any certain scents or tastes that bring back memories for you? It's funny how the brain works that way. A particular aroma can meet your nose and flood your heart with emotions. Or a specific spice can hit your tongue and overflow your mind with recollections of your childhood. One of those things for me is cocktail sauce, which reminds me of New Year's Eve. When I was growing up, we always celebrated the new year. We had our own mini party at home for which my parents would set out trays of food. I remember one particular round tray that had six sections for different foods, such as pickles, olives, cheese, pickled herring (which I bypassed), and a variety of other foods. We always had lentil soup as well because it was a tradition on my mother's side of the family. The food that I recall the most, though, is the shrimp with cocktail sauce. Anytime I eat cocktail sauce with my shrimp now, I am inundated with memories of New Year's.

I always love starting a new year. It feels like a clean slate, a blank page, a fresh start. A new year is an excellent opportunity to make changes in your life and paint a beautiful future for yourself. (Some people prefer to view their birthday as a new year and a fresh start, which is a fabulous idea as well.) When it comes to New Year's, we hear a lot of talk about resolutions. We see countless commercials for exercise equipment, diet programs, and weight loss shakes, all aimed to people resolving to get in better shape. I admit, since I love New Year's so much, I like resolutions as well. Unfortunately, though, many resolutions fizzle out before we turn our calendars over to February.

This is one of the reasons why some people prefer picking a word to get them through the year. They pick one word that represents something they would like to focus on for the year, and they keep this word in the forefront of their mind each day. Some example words are: peace, strength, healing, Jesus, love, brave, and so on. There have even been entire books written on the subject of picking one word for the year.

Picking a word for the year is something I have enjoyed doing myself many times. One particular year I chose the word *seek* because I wanted to seek the Lord more.

Of course, seeking the Lord is a lifelong practice, but during this season, I felt I could use a boost in my spiritual walk. I had many distractions in my life that kept me from growing in God as much as I wanted. I admit that some of these distractions were self-imposed, so that is one reason why I felt the word *seek* was appropriate. It would help me to make better choices in my daily life. My hope was that it would help me to remember to lay aside any unnecessary obstacles that were in my way. I also felt this word would help me keep my priorities in order. I wanted to be more intentional about seeking God and walking closely with Him.

Jeremiah 29:13 says, "You will seek me and find me when you seek me with all your heart." Seeking God is a vital part of giving Him our whole heart. So many things go awry when we don't. Other priorities creep into our lives to replace God. We will wind up doing our own thing and not His will. We lack the peace that surpasses understanding. We are unable to properly handle trials that come our way. We don't have true contentment in life. We can become stuck in negative patterns. Big decisions can cripple us. And we don't learn and grow in our walk with the Lord.

Seeking Improves Our Listening

Failure to seek after God creates disorder in our lives because intentionally seeking God is imperative for hearing His voice. If our minds are cluttered with other things, then how can we expect to hear the voice of the Lord in the midst of the chaos? We need to clear away the noise to hear Him.

As I mentioned in an earlier chapter, my husband and I enjoy spotting wildlife in the mountains. However, seeing an animal isn't enough for us. We also try to capture a picture of each animal we see. Photography helps us to remember and relive each moment. At the end of each calendar year, we like to put together an album of our best pictures from that year. It can be difficult to weed through thousands of pictures and narrow them down to our best, but admittedly, not all the photos we take turn out well. Many are dark or blurry. When we're out in a wooded area dense with trees, there is a lot of natural shade, which can make the pictures dark. But what's worse, in my opinion, is the greenery. Often when we spot a bear in the midst of the woods, the many leaves and bushes in front of him and behind him confuse the camera. The camera doesn't always know what to focus on when there are too many items in its view, so it might focus on some of the leaves that are closest to it, causing the bear behind them to turn out blurry.

This happened to us recently and unfortunately it made us miss a great shot. There was a mom bear and three cubs walking through the forest, heading away from us. But one of the cubs was curious to see my husband, who was taking a picture of him, so he turned around and came back. What was especially cute was that he was between two trees and peeked over a bush that stood between the trees to see what was going on. It would have been a masterpiece photo, except the camera didn't know what to focus on. It tried to focus on some of the greenery, and the cub turned out blurry.

I think this is how we operate too. In this fast-paced world we live in, we don't always know what to focus on. We have too many things vying for our attention: email, text messages, social media, television, radio, video games, tasks at work, to-do lists at home, the needs of our loved ones, etc. It can be overwhelming and cause us to lose focus. All the noise of the world quickly and easily drowns out the voice of the Lord.

It isn't just the world, though. When we get alone and turn all those things off, we are still blasted with our own thoughts. When we pray, we tend to rattle off all of our requests. Do we ever stop and take the time to listen to what God might have to say to us? It can be very difficult to quiet our minds, but we have to clear the noise in our lives in order to better hear the voice of God.

If we are purposeful when it comes to quieting our minds and listening to God, we can see success in this area. It won't come on its own, so we have to intentionally emphasize this in our daily lives. This is something I have been working on in my own life. As a result, it has helped me feel more peaceful and joyful. Most of all, I am amazed at how much more I hear from God, when I actually seek to hear from Him.

Ways to Hear from the Lord

Hearing God's voice is something I have heard many Christians say they struggle with. If we don't hear an audible voice, we might think that God is not speaking to us. But I do believe God speaks to His children, if we take the time to listen.

We already talked about the importance of reading your Bible. This is a vital avenue for hearing God's voice. When we make reading the Bible a habit, it helps us to recognize the sound of God's voice because the Bible is the breathing, living Word of God. Reading the Bible daily causes our hearts to become tethered to Him, and this in turn helps us to feel His breathing, life-giving presence in every situation. As it says in John 10:27, "My sheep listen to my voice; I know them, and they follow me." Intentionally listening for God's voice during your Bible reading time, is the perfect way to start trying to hear from Him. Before you begin reading, pray and ask Him to speak to you through His Word. Also, keep a journal handy so you can write down anything He impresses on your heart.

Don't be mistaken, though; God is not only present during the reading of His Word. God is everywhere. If we merely pay attention, we will hear from Him. Our lives are very distracted. Even when we're in the middle of an important task our minds are often elsewhere. Therefore, we have to be deliberate about paying more attention to what is going on around us. When we do, we will hear different things the Lord is trying to tell us. Many times we think something is just a coincidence when it is really God speaking to us. For example, if I hear the same Bible verse from several different sources in a matter of days, I will tune in to hear what God might be saying to me.

Another way we hear from God is through the Holy Spirit. When we became Christians, the Holy Spirit came to live on the inside of us. Jesus said in John 14:26, "But the Advocate, the Holy Spirit, whom the Father will send in my name, will teach you all things and will remind you of everything I have said to you." With the Holy Spirit living inside of us, we have discernment. We might get a feeling in the pit of our stomach warning us against something or leading us in a certain direction. Many times that is from the Holy Spirit.

Inviting the Lord to speak to you is another way to hear from Him. This is something I have been trying to do more and more. When you do this, it is best to eliminate distractions, which means that choosing where and when you want to sit with the Lord is important. In my home, there is a place I often go when I want to read my Bible, pray, or just listen for God's voice: my closet. My husband and even my dogs know that when they haven't seen me in a while, they can probably find me in my closet. I even do a lot of writing in there because it frees me from distractions. I am hypersensitive to various noises such as talking, typing, television, and music, so when I am searching for peace and quiet, my closet is my favorite place to go.

There are a couple other places that also work well for me. I find myself in the quiet of my car almost daily. I actually can't avoid my car, since I have to drive to work. If you spend a lot of time driving, try turning off the radio and quieting your mind. Or if you have a full-time job, another option is to sit in your car on your lunch break for ten to twenty minutes. No radio, no cell phone, no other distractions.

I often seek God when I'm outdoors too. I might go for a stroll around my yard or just sit quietly in a chair. I always feel closer to God when I'm out in nature with no walls between me and the sky above. Try it and see if it has the same effect on you.

Once you find a good place and time that works for you, invite the Lord to speak to you. You can say something like, "Lord, is there anything you would like to say to me? If there is anything you want to tell me, here I am." Then purposefully sit quietly and wait on the Lord to speak to you.

Once you are intentional about seeking the Lord and listening for His voice, you will be amazed at how He begins to show up in unexpected ways.

Reflection

Do you intentionally seek God with your whole heart? If not, how can you begin to do so?

_____

_____

_____

_____

_____

Is hearing from the Lord something that comes easily for you, or is it more difficult? If you find it difficult, can you incorporate some of the tips in this chapter into your daily life?

_____

_____

_____

_____

Take a few moments now to sit quietly, clear the clutter from your mind, and invite the Lord to speak to you.

_____

_____

_____

_____

_____

Chapter 5 – Living Water

A few years back, my sister and brother-in-law were out of town with some other family members on my brother-in-law's side. They all decided to go somewhere for dinner. Since there was a big group of them, they drove in separate vehicles. My brother-in-law and sister were to follow another vehicle in their party. Everything was going fine along the drive, until the vehicle they were following pulled over to the side of the road. My brother-in-law and sister pulled over as well, and to their horror, a man who they didn't recognize got out of the car in front of them. He asked, "Why are you following me?" Apparently, at some point they got into traffic and my brother-in-law accidentally followed the wrong car.

This story makes me laugh. However, it also makes me think about us and our walk with the Lord. Sometimes we follow what appears to be the right thing in life, when in reality it could be something leading us down the wrong road, away from God. Or perhaps we might have outside influences distracting us from the correct path, such as the traffic that my brother-in-law and sister got into. We wind up getting off track, due to various outside forces. And in the end we wind up lost. That is why it is so important to keep our attention on God. He will not lead us astray and He will not let us get lost. He will keep us fulfilled, and as a result outside distractions won't tempt us to follow the wrong path.

An Empty Cup

My husband and I enjoy going to baseball games. We love the sport and love certain teams in particular. My husband was born in Gainesville, Florida, so the Florida Gators are one of our teams. It can be exhilarating to watch them work hard and succeed with a win. At one recent Gators game that we went to, our team was losing to the Tennessee Volunteers 9-2. Yet inning by inning the Gators chipped away at the wall in front of them and wound up winning 10-9. What an exciting victory to watch!

Unfortunately, there is something else I remember from that game. It's not something we saw at this game alone but rather something we see at many of the games. We often see people in the stands who are not even watching the game. Instead, they are scrolling through their social media feeds on their smartphones. And it's not just young kids like you might think. There are many middle-aged people who do this as well. Looking around at all these people makes us feel sad. An increasing number of people would rather look at something fake on a screen than the real life that is happening right in front of them.

There was another incident that occurred around this same time as that Gators–Volunteers game. My husband and I were in the post office. It was very quiet, with only one person in line ahead of us. This meant that there wasn't a long wait. In spite of this fact, that one person ahead of us scrolled through his Facebook feed while standing in line. What's worse is that he even *continued to scroll when he was up at the counter*! My husband and I were shocked. The incident was actually very distressing to us, as it reflected how our society is these days.

These incidents hit home and prompted me to go through a fast that included deleting several applications from my phone that I felt were taking up too much of my time. When we think of fasting, we usually think of refraining from eating. However, fasting can be refraining from any number of things. I have heard people talk about fasting from things such as the news, complaining, and devices. Fasting can be done for various reasons. We might fast in order to grow in our spiritual walk. We might fast when we are standing in prayer over a big concern in our lives. Or we might fast when we are uncertain about a big decision we are facing. In my case, I felt there were things that were keeping me from drawing closer to God. Therefore, I decided to fast from them.

I used to love hours of peace and quiet. Years ago I could take a four-hour drive, by myself, without even turning on the radio. My mother would ask me if I got bored. My answer was that this quiet time was glorious, just me and God.

Then in May of 2012 I purchased my first smartphone. (I remember exactly when it was because it was the same day my husband had his pre-op appointment for his neck surgery.) After I got the smartphone, everything pretty much went downhill after that. If I was just sitting and waiting, I would feel the need to do something to pass the time. I would check email, social media sites, or play a game. At times I almost felt desperate as I searched for anything to satisfy a deep thirst within me. However, I often walked away feeling even thirstier than before.

Devices aren't the only distractions in our lives. Think of different things in your life that you reach for on a daily or weekly basis. Your smartphone or tablet, social media, email, books, television, video games, food, alcohol, medications, shopping, and so on.

Too much of these things can keep us from experiencing life, affect our relationships, and ultimately prevent us from fully seeking God with our whole heart. We go through our daily routines without giving these things much thought. They're just items we've grown accustomed to. But if they take time away from God and prevent us from giving Him our whole heart, then they are a distraction.

Let's take this a step further. Sometimes these "distractions" are really security blankets to us, and we might not even realize it. Sometimes we tend to reach for these things either to give us an escape from the real world or to give us instant gratification. That is, we reach for them to satisfy something inside of us that only God can truly satisfy. It's like reaching for an empty cup, when Jesus is the only one who can truly quench our thirst.

Keeping God in First Place

Some of the things that we reach for aren't necessarily bad things. Sometimes they are even considered good things. Yet they can become a problem when we let these items take the front row in our lives. If we put these things in first place in our lives, then they have become idols or gods to us.

In Exodus 20:3, God says, "You shall have no other gods before me." At the time when this was written, the nations surrounding Israel worshipped their own man-made gods, which were really not gods at all, for there is only one true God. So we might be quick to think that this verse doesn't pertain to us because we don't worship other gods as we read about in the Old Testament, but it very much does pertain to us. Anything that we put above God is an idol. Money, other people, ourselves, success, status, relationships, alcohol, drugs, video games, television, food, social media, what other people think of us, our job, shopping, our car, our marriage, our children, our home. All these things and more can become idols to us. Often times we don't even realize how deeply we are treasuring them.

That is why it is especially important to keep our eyes on the Lord. If we don't seek God, then we will seek other things to replace Him. God should be included in every area of our lives. He will help us to stay on course. He will keep our hearts in check. He will satisfy our needs. All of these other things might give us some sort of boost in the moment, but they will not keep us fulfilled.

Quenching Your Thirst

When my husband and I want to go to a baseball game, we usually opt for a night game because of the cooler temperatures. We do live in Florida, after all. There are times, though, when we do wind up going to a game in the afternoon or midday. That blazing sun can be brutal at those games. We have seen other fans pass out and the paramedics come to their aid. The people in charge at the ballpark do all they can to keep the fans taken care of. They have a huge pump of sun screen that you can use for free, a couple of stations with oscillating misting fans, and free cups of ice. My husband and I try to stay hydrated. We drink sports drinks or water and take up the offer of ice to chew on, which seems to give us the most relief. However, all of these things only help while we are consuming them. Once the drink or the ice is gone, we're back to feeling miserable, hot, and weak.

The same is true with all the things we reach for in our lives, isn't it? They only satisfy us for the moment. Then when that moment has passed, we are thirsty again. If I turn to worldly things, I will never quench my thirst. I will never be truly satisfied. I will not find true fulfillment. Nothing in this world can make my heart content. But Jesus provided a beautiful promise. It is found in John 4:4-26, which recounts a detour He took to meet with a woman on His way to Galilee:

> *Now he had to go through Samaria. So he came to a town in Samaria called Sychar, near the plot of ground Jacob had given to his son Joseph. Jacob's well was there, and Jesus, tired as he was from the journey, sat down by the well. It was about noon.*

> *When a Samaritan woman came to draw water, Jesus said to her, "Will you give me a drink?" (His disciples had gone into the town to buy food.)*

> *The Samaritan woman said to him, "You are a Jew and I am a Samaritan woman. How can you ask me for a drink?" (For Jews do not associate with Samaritans.)*

> *Jesus answered her, "If you knew the gift of God and who it is that asks you for a drink, you would have asked him and he would have given you living water."*

"Sir," the woman said, "you have nothing to draw with and the well is deep. Where can you get this living water? Are you greater than our father Jacob, who gave us the well and drank from it himself, as did also his sons and his livestock?"

Jesus answered, "Everyone who drinks this water will be thirsty again, but whoever drinks the water I give them will never thirst. Indeed, the water I give them will become in them a spring of water welling up to eternal life."

The woman said to him, "Sir, give me this water so that I won't get thirsty and have to keep coming here to draw water."

He told her, "Go, call your husband and come back."

"I have no husband," she replied.

Jesus said to her, "You are right when you say you have no husband. The fact is, you have had five husbands, and the man you now have is not your husband. What you have just said is quite true."

"Sir," the woman said, "I can see that you are a prophet. Our ancestors worshiped on this mountain, but you Jews claim that the place where we must worship is in Jerusalem."

"Woman," Jesus replied, "believe me, a time is coming when you will worship the Father neither on this mountain nor in Jerusalem. You Samaritans worship what you do not know; we worship what we do know, for salvation is from the Jews. Yet a time is coming and has now come when the true worshipers will worship the Father in the Spirit and in truth, for they are the kind of worshipers the Father seeks. God is spirit, and his worshipers must worship in the Spirit and in truth."

The woman said, "I know that Messiah" (called Christ) "is coming. When he comes, he will explain everything to us."

Then Jesus declared, "I, the one speaking to you—I am he."

This is a beautiful passage that illustrates how only Jesus can truly satisfy us. When we turn to the Lord, we will find true fulfillment in life. I have seen in my own life how this is true. In the past, I have allowed a great number of things to keep me from God; I have tried to satisfy my thirst with them instead of Him. But only when I laid those things down and put God first and foremost in my life, only when I truly gave Him my whole heart, did my life change for the better.

The same is true for you. Perhaps you have things in your life that you reach for that always leave you feeling empty. Jesus is the answer. Jesus promised that if we turn to Him, we will never thirst again.

Reflection

List out all of the things that you can think of that you reach for on a daily or weekly basis. Also make a list of your hobbies and activities that take up some of your time. List all of the things in your life that you love, such as your spouse, your children, your family, your home, your job, your car, money, and food. And finally, list some of your goals, things you would like to accomplish.

_____

_____

_____

_____

_____

Go through each of these items one by one. Do you feel that any of them equate to your happiness? Ask yourself, are you willing to live without any of these things, if it is the Lord's will? Is it possible that any of these things are more important to you than Jesus?

_____

_____

_____

_____

If you have discovered that there are items in your life that you have been seeking to quench your thirst, would you consider prayerfully laying it aside for a time and seeking the Lord instead?

_____

_____

_____

_____

Chapter 6 – Working for the Kingdom of God

Have you noticed how popular sloths have become recently? Everywhere you turn, you will see sloths. Stuffed animals, pillows, tumblers, plaques, jewelry, purses, and so on. I don't really understand this infatuation. Sloths are known for being extremely slow. Does this mean that there are a lot of lazy people in our culture today? Or are these people tired of our fast-paced world and envy the sloth? I was recently told by a fellow writer that she found sloths to be cute. Perhaps that is all there is to it for most people. Even so, I found it funny when I stumbled across a Bible verse that mentions the famous attribute of this creature.

In Romans 12:11, it is said that we should be "not slothful in business; fervent in spirit; serving the Lord" (KJV). As I dug further, I found there are actually numerous Bible verses where slothfulness is frowned upon. Slothful means lazy. Therefore, the Bible is basically telling us not to be lazy. Romans 12:11 is talking specifically about not being lazy when serving the Lord.

There are numerous Bible verses regarding work, serving, helping others, and being good stewards. And In Mark 10:45, Jesus says of Himself, "For even the Son of Man did not come to be served, but to serve, and to give his life as a ransom for many." If Jesus came to serve, then shouldn't we serve as well? When we read the Bible, it becomes clear that when we give God our whole heart, working for Him, serving Him, and serving others are all important tasks. We are working for the kingdom of God in everything we do.

Now let me clear up one thing before we go any further. Working for the kingdom of God is not a way of gaining God's approval or acceptance. God already loves you more than you can imagine. He can't love you more than He already does. Ephesians 2:8-9 says, "For it is by grace you have been saved, through faith—and this is not from yourselves, it is the gift of God— not by works, so that no one can boast."

Our work comes from a place of love. We love the Lord so much, that we want to do things for His glory and His kingdom, to honor Him. We want to be good to other people in order to illustrate the love of the Lord. We might be the only reflection of Jesus that some people see in their day...or in their lifetimes. So we should take every opportunity to be a good reflection of Him.

Start Wherever You Are

Working for the kingdom of God might look different for each of us because we all have our own unique gifts and we are all in different seasons of life. We can't all be pastors and missionaries, but we can still work for the kingdom of God. My opinion is that all Christians are in ministry. Our ministry might be at home, at church, at work, or at the grocery store. We might serve our family, friends, coworkers, or even strangers. Wherever we find ourselves at any given moment is where we have an opportunity to work for the kingdom of God. Wherever you go, you have the power of the Holy Spirit within you and you can thus make a positive impact on those you encounter. Whatever you do today, you can be a shining light in a dark world.

If you are a working person, then you can begin there. The Bible says in Colossians 3:23-24, "Whatever you do, work at it with all your heart, as working for the Lord, not for human masters, since you know that you will receive an inheritance from the Lord as a reward. It is the Lord Christ you are serving." Although a certain company signs our paychecks, God is our true boss and the true source of our income. When we remember this as we enter the buildings where we work each day, it gives us a new perspective. When a dreaded task is handed to us, we will take it more willingly. When a coworker directs harsh words at us, we will be able to shrug it off. And we will put more effort into our jobs with joy and with a smile.

Let me give you a good example. My husband, Mickey, and I used to work for the same company, so I saw first-hand how he was an excellent model of someone who worked for the kingdom of God. Before my husband retired, everyone always knew that if they needed to get something, they could rely on him. Even when it was something that was not part of his actual job duties, he would figure out what needed to be done. And he never left a job half-way completed. If someone asked for his help, he would help, end of story. When he saw trash that someone had left behind, he would pick it up and throw it away. Mickey always left a place better than he found it. And he still does! For example, any time we go to the store, if he sees shopping carts strewn about the parking lot, he will push some of them to the corral or up to the store.

My husband is naturally a friendly and humorous person, so he felt it was his mission to help his coworkers laugh and smile during their day. We worked for a health organization, so Mickey wouldn't only deal with fellow employees; he encountered patients in his day as well. Therefore, his helpful attitude also extended to the patients. When he saw a sick patient who was waiting for a ride outdoors, he would get that person a chair to sit in and make them more comfortable until their ride arrived. I could relay countless stories of how my husband has a heart for Lord and shows it through serving. He is the epitome of integrity, and he loves to help other people. Over the years, Mickey has taught me a lot about working for the kingdom of God. Even when he doesn't feel like it, even when he is busy, he still takes the time to help someone else.

Whether we are at work, at home, or at church, anywhere we go, we too can have this attitude if we keep in the forefront of our minds that we are working for the kingdom of God and the Lord is our boss. Start by doing a good job at whatever task is in front of you and by keeping a positive attitude. People around you will see you smile and they will be affected by it. Just by being kind to others we can have a positive impact on their lives.

When my husband was in the hospital for neck surgery a few years ago, many people were in and out of his room. One of the people I remember the most from his stay in the hospital, though, was the lady who delivered his tray of food. This might not seem like the most influential job, but it was like a ray of sunshine came in the room with this lady. She was positive and upbeat, with a big smile on her face. This lady knew she had an opportunity to positively impact all the sick and hurting patients she encountered.

The Love of Jesus

Spreading the love of Jesus is our objective when it comes to working for the kingdom of God. Jesus says in John 13:34-35, "A new command I give you: Love one another. As I have loved you, so you must love one another. By this everyone will know that you are my disciples, if you love one another."

My husband's aforementioned neck surgery was done at the same health organization that we worked for. I sat in the waiting room all day. In fact, I was scared to leave the waiting room, because I figured the moment I did, the staff would try to get a hold of me to give me an update on my husband. Thankfully, everything went well and then they finally admitted my husband to a room to stay overnight. I would stay with him there, and make a bed of the recliner in the room. This part of the story probably doesn't sound overly exceptional to you. I believe most of you would do the same for your loved ones and probably have.

But there is a third person in this story I want to tell you about: my friend and former coworker. She kept in contact with me throughout the day to see how things were going. She knew I had stayed in the waiting room for hours and therefore had not eaten anything all day. So, in the early evening hours she called me and told me to go downstairs to the main door of the hospital. She had driven across town, without asking me, and just showed up with food. She had brought me a bowl of spaghetti that she had made for her own family's dinner that night. What my sweet friend did that day still fills me with awe, and I believe that her actions made the Lord happy as well.

However, my friend's kindness wasn't a one-time thing. Fast forward a couple of years to when my husband had another procedure. I was in the same waiting room, by myself, awaiting news. Since my friend worked at the same place that my husband and I did, her office was just across the street, and my friend used her lunch break to sit by my side in the waiting room. In our society today, we don't often see this kind of selfless giving. Most people don't want to even give away five minutes of their time, let alone their whole lunch break. Serving your loved ones, your friends, and those around you is a beautiful way of spreading the love of Jesus.

I understand that things like this might come more naturally to some people than they do to others. Some people are extroverted and can easily put themselves out there. I personally am an introvert and often shy away from unusual situations. However, if we are willing to take a step out of our comfort zone, the reward will be worth it.

Let me share an example. They say it is better to give than to receive. And isn't it true? Giving someone that perfect gift can fill us with much more excitement than opening a gift ourselves. One December I stopped at a local gas station and the cashier oohed and aahed over my Christmas purse. It was red with a green, plaid bow. She mentioned that her daughter would love it, since she had recently acquired an interest in purses. I asked how old her daughter was and she said ten. We chatted for a few more minutes about it before I headed home. What that lady didn't know was that I just so happened to have a second purse like mine at home that I had never used. I wanted to give this purse away, but because I loved it so much, I wanted it to go to the perfect home. Now I had an idea. I'm sure you know where this is going. I wanted to give the second purse to the cashier for her daughter.

I mulled over the idea on the drive home. My initial thought was to go back to the gas station another day. But how was I to know what days and times this lady worked? Perhaps we wouldn't cross paths again until weeks later. By then, Christmas would be over, and a red-and-green purse wouldn't be as meaningful. Plus, due to my introverted nature, I typically shied away from these sorts of interactions, so I wasn't sure that I would actually return for this purpose at a later date. I knew I very well might talk myself out of it. Therefore, I decided it was best to just do it that day if I was going to do it at all.

I went home, retrieved the twin purse, and went straight back to the store. The lady was so delighted and raved about how much her daughter would love the purse. What was even more astonishing was how ecstatic it made me as I headed home for a second time that day. Working for the kingdom of God and helping others will not only benefit the other person, but it floods our hearts with joy too. Let's take a look at a biblical example in Luke 5:17-26.

> *One day Jesus was teaching, and Pharisees and teachers of the law were sitting there. They had come from every village of Galilee and from Judea and Jerusalem. And the power of the Lord was with*

Jesus to heal the sick. Some men came carrying a paralyzed man on a mat and tried to take him into the house to lay him before Jesus. When they could not find a way to do this because of the crowd, they went up on the roof and lowered him on his mat through the tiles into the middle of the crowd, right in front of Jesus.

When Jesus saw their faith, he said, "Friend, your sins are forgiven."

The Pharisees and the teachers of the law began thinking to themselves, "Who is this fellow who speaks blasphemy? Who can forgive sins but God alone?"

Jesus knew what they were thinking and asked, "Why are you thinking these things in your hearts? Which is easier: to say, 'Your sins are forgiven,' or to say, 'Get up and walk'? But I want you to know that the Son of Man has authority on earth to forgive sins." So he said to the paralyzed man, "I tell you, get up, take your mat and go home." Immediately he stood up in front of them, took what he had been lying on and went home praising God. Everyone was amazed and gave praise to God.

They were filled with awe and said, "We have seen remarkable things today."

There are two things I want to point out in this story. First of all, this story is just one of numerous examples of how Jesus helped others. Jesus didn't tell the paralyzed man that He was too busy to help him that day. He didn't tell him that He was in the middle of teaching. He didn't tell him to come back another day. Jesus always made those around Him a priority. Jesus was selfless and loving, always. When He walked the earth, Jesus looked out for others. He helped anyone He could, He healed all those who were sick, and He spread love everywhere He went. Jesus should be our role model and who we try to be more like in our earthly walk.

I also want to point out the friends of the paralyzed man. The place was too crowded for them to bring the man through the door. *So they climbed on top of the roof to lower the man down!* This just blows me away. How many people do you know who would do that? Most people today would just say something like, "Sorry, man, we can't get in. We tried. Today is not your day. Maybe some other time." But these men decided to do whatever it would take to help their friend and they didn't allow anything to stop them.

This story really makes me reflect on my own behaviors. Would I be that tenacious to help a friend in need? Would I do whatever it took? I hope that we all would. Imagine how beautiful the world would be if we all remembered that we were working for the kingdom of God, if we all served the Lord with our whole heart, if we all were kind to those around us, and if we all spread the love of Jesus. I think we would see miracles take place.

Reflection

Make a list of your talents, gifts, and interests.

_____

_____

_____

_____

_____

Considering this list, in what ways can you serve the Lord with your whole heart?

_____

_____

_____

_____

What changes can you make when you are at home, at work, at church, or at any other place you go to spread the love of Jesus?

_____

_____

_____

_____

Chapter 7 – Trusting God

In order to give God our whole heart, we have to trust Him. It's just like with any other relationship. If we don't trust someone, then we won't be completely open with that person. Think of different people in your life such as your spouse, your children, your parents, your siblings, your friends, your coworkers, and your acquaintances. With some of those people, you might share struggles you are dealing with, victories you have achieved, dreams you are hoping for, deep hurts you have endured, or even just small tidbits of your daily life. Yet there are other people in your life you would never share any of that with. Part of this is likely because you haven't established trust within those relationships.

The same is true with God. Picture this: You walk up to the shore and allow the ocean to skim your toes. Then when the tide gets a little higher, you take a step back. You aren't willing to allow your whole body to get wet. You are afraid that once the water completely covers your feet and climbs up your legs, the sand that you are standing on will become unstable. You could start to sink, or worse, you might be swept away. There is nothing for you to grab hold of. You believe that no one and nothing can truly save you. Therefore, you play it safe, moving away from the shore, keeping that water just out of reach.

This is how we are with God at times. We keep Him at arm's length. On the outside it might appear that we have a strong relationship with Him. But on the inside we know that our faith is not on solid ground. When He asks us to do something that makes us feel uncomfortable or insecure, we take a step back. We cannot seem to put our full trust in Him.

God is Good

What is the root cause that is keeping you from trusting God? For many people, it is that they have experienced pain and disappointment in life, which has caused them to doubt God's goodness. We all have had to deal with hurts in our lives. But the truth is that, even in the midst of suffering, God is still good. Always.

In the beginning, when God created the world, everything He made was perfect. God does not make mistakes.

However, God did give mankind free will. No loving parent wants to tie their children down and control their every move. They want their children to step out into the world, learn new things, and experience life. So it was with God. Unfortunately, in the book of Genesis chapter 3, we see that Adam and Eve were deceived by the devil and made a mistake by breaking the command that the Lord had given them. You are probably familiar with the story in Genesis 3:1-7:

> Now the serpent was more crafty than any of the wild animals the Lord God had made. He said to the woman, "Did God really say, 'You must not eat from any tree in the garden'?"

> The woman said to the serpent, "We may eat fruit from the trees in the garden, but God did say, 'You must not eat fruit from the tree that is in the middle of the garden, and you must not touch it, or you will die.'"

> "You will not certainly die," the serpent said to the woman. "For God knows that when you eat from it your eyes will be opened, and you will be like God, knowing good and evil."

When the woman saw that the fruit of the tree was good for food and pleasing to the eye, and also desirable for gaining wisdom, she took some and ate it. She also gave some to her husband, who was with her, and he ate it. Then the eyes of both of them were opened, and they realized they were naked; so they sewed fig leaves together and made coverings for themselves.

That is when sin entered the world. Along with sin came suffering, pain, sorrow, and death. So one thing we have to remember when dealing with pain in our lives is the true source. The enemy is the one who brought pain into this world.

In John 10:10, Jesus says, "The thief comes only to steal and kill and destroy; I have come that they may have life, and have it to the full." The thief that Jesus is talking about is Satan. He has brought death and destruction to this world we live in. Yet at times when bad things happen, people are quick to blame it on God.

If you have ever read the Bible from cover to cover, you have seen how mankind kept messing up through history. It was a constant battle. They sinned, they turned from God, they fell into deep pits of evil, they followed their own wicked pleasures, and at times they even blamed God for their problems. Yet God still loved His children so much and wanted to see them saved. That is why He sent Jesus to die for all of our sins. Even though His children turned their backs on Him, He still paved a way to save them. How can we not trust a God who loves us *that* much?

Fear is another reason why we might not trust God. Fear causes us to try to keep things from Him. Of course we know that God is omniscient. He sees everything and He knows everything. But do we still attempt to hide things from Him? At times we might try to keep our true feelings and emotions hidden. Or perhaps we tuck away some of our dreams and desires or try to bury our pasts and conceal our scars. Maybe we think that if we bring some of these things to God it will stir up too much pain or that if we are too open with the Lord He might strike us down.

Some of these reactions stem from our relationships with humans. When we put our hearts on the line with people, we often get hurt. If we share our dreams with our loved ones, they might shoot us down and tell us all the reasons why it won't work. People are quick to judge others and point fingers. It can be hard for humans to extend grace and mercy. Our heavenly Father isn't like that, though. God is love and He loves His children. He cares about His children's feelings. His children's hopes and dreams matter to Him. God knows how we are feeling even when we don't come out and tell Him. Our Father won't harm us for being honest with Him.

And then there is control. The need to surrender control is another reason why people might not trust God. Many of us are used to handling life on our own, and so the thought of allowing someone else to take over and steer can cause a bit of panic. Personally, I have anxiety when I think something could go wrong. I often imagine the worst-case scenario in my mind and feel a bit short of breath. Whether I am worried about a family member who is traveling, or worrying about a hurricane that is headed our way, I have a tendency to worry. I want to control things so that I know everyone is safe. In these situations, something that helps me is to say aloud over and over, "I trust You, God. I trust You, God." When I do this, my fears calm down. I can grab hold of God's hand and allow His peace to settle inside of me.

Learning to Trust

When I was a senior in high school, rather than taking a traditional physical education class, I took one that focused on trust. This had me participating in many fun activities throughout the school year. My class had opportunities to do things such as go rock climbing and walk on a tight rope twenty-five feet above the ground. With each task we had to rely on our teacher and our fellow students to keep us safe. For example, when we went rock climbing, we each had someone down below holding our ropes. The term for it is "belaying." If the climber falls, the person belaying can pull on the rope to lock the climber in place and keep them from hitting the ground. For another activity, we students stood on the ground near the bleachers and formed two lines facing each other. We all stuck our arms forward to make a platform of sorts, and then one student went up on top of the bleachers, turned their back to the rest of us down below, and fell backwards into our arms.

Each of these activities was a roller coaster of emotions. Initially the student might feel fear and anxiety. They might find it hard to trust other people with their life and they might not trust their own capabilities to complete the task. As they followed through, though, their emotions would turn to confidence. They saw that they could, in fact, do better than they had initially imagined and that their fellow students would not let them down. Then afterwards they would feel exhilarated. With their classmates' help, they had done it! They had completed the task, and everything went far better than they'd assumed it would.

This reminds me of our trust in God. We might be scared to take the initial step. The thought of relinquishing control makes us want to panic. But finally, we decide to let go. We take one step toward the Lord. Then another. As we continue to climb, our confidence builds. We see that God is there by our side, every step of the way. And in the end, we have joy because things went far better with God than they might have without Him. Our joy settles into peace as we realize we have nothing to worry about with God Almighty holding onto our hand.

Hannah

I was recently reading the story of Hannah in 1 Samuel chapter 1. In case you're not familiar with Hannah, here's the scoop: There was a man named Elkanah who had two wives, Hannah and Peninnah. Peninnah had many children, but Hannah had none. Peninnah would taunt Hannah about this fact, and it upset Hannah because bearing children was especially important during those days.

However, on one of the family's yearly trips to worship and sacrifice to the Lord at Shiloh, things took a turn. Hannah was very distressed and would not eat. She prayed, pouring her heart out to the Lord. 1 Samuel 1:10-11 says:

> *In her deep anguish Hannah prayed to the Lord, weeping bitterly. And she made a vow, saying, "Lord Almighty, if you will only look on your servant's misery and remember me, and not forget your servant but give her a son, then I will give him to the Lord for all the days of his life, and no razor will ever be used on his head."*

Eli the priest was nearby. He and Hannah spoke to one another briefly, and once Hannah explained what she had been doing, Eli said to her, "Go in peace, and may the God of Israel grant you what you have asked of him." Hannah replied, "May your servant find favor in your eyes." The Bible records that after this "she went her way and ate something, and her face was no longer downcast" (1 Samuel 1:17-18). In time, Hannah did have several children. The first-born was a son named Samuel who became a great prophet of Israel.

Something about Hannah's story struck me. One moment the Bible says she was weeping bitterly and would not eat; then soon after, it says that her face was no longer downcast and she ate something. It seems like such a quick shift. However, I believe that within this shift, Hannah made a decision to trust God, and in coming to the decision to trust, Hannah also went through a transition. Let's break this transition down into five steps, which are easy to remember because they spell out the word TRUST:

T – Tell God what's on your heart
R – Request His help
U – Understand that He is in control
S – Stop worrying
T – Tell God you trust Him

T – Tell God what's on your heart
The Bible says that Hannah prayed to the Lord. We already talked about the importance of prayer. Well, this story illustrates how bringing our heart to God in prayer is an important step when we are dealing with any adversity in our lives. Prayer is also a significant step for putting our trust in God.

R – Request His help
Hannah asked God for a child. When we learn to trust God, we realize that He is our source for anything and everything that we may want and need in life.

U – Understand that He is in control

When we bring our requests to the Lord, we have to remember that we might not always get what we want. Yet when we trust Him, we have a deep conviction "that in all things God works for the good of those who love him, who have been called according to his purpose" (Romans 8:28).

S – Stop worrying

Many of us have a habit of praying for things, yet we still worry about what we prayed for. We say that we will hand our problems over to God, but in reality we hang onto them. We think that we need to hold our issues tightly in our fists. It seems that Hannah simply got up from her prayer, without any more worries on her heart. When we pray for things and hand them over to God, we also have to stop worrying about them.

T – Tell God you trust Him

As I mentioned earlier, sometimes I will verbally tell God that I trust Him. In this case, I feel Hannah did the same with her actions, rather than her words. Initially she would not eat. However, after praying, she did eat. She was moving on and allowing God to work out the problem on her behalf.

This story had an impact on me and caused me to want to trust God more. Trust that He is a good God. Trust that if I don't get what I want, then that means He must have a better plan in mind. Trust that when things go wrong, He will still work it for good.

Each morning when I get up, I want to place my trust in the hands of the Lord. When we trust Him, we will see His love for us on a whole new level. We will see that He has our best interests in mind, and we will be able to follow His lead. As Scripture says in Psalm 143:8, "Let the morning bring me word of your unfailing love, for I have put my trust in you. Show me the way I should go, for to you I entrust my life."

Trusting God is a choice. Either we choose to believe His Word, including His promises found in the Bible or we don't. What will you choose?

Reflection

Do you have any past hurts in your life that have kept you from believing that God is good? Going forward, let's try to remember what it says in John 10:10: "The thief comes only to steal and kill and destroy; I have come that they may have life, and have it to the full."

_____

_____

_____

_____

_____

Make a list of all the pieces of your life that you find it difficult to trust God with, such as your family, your dreams, your heart, and your goals.

_____

_____

_____

_____

One by one, go through each item you wrote down and tell the Lord, "God, I trust You with _____."

_____

_____

_____

_____

_____

Chapter 8 – Allowing God to Lead

One day I had to attend a meeting across town, so I planned to go through a drive-through for some much-needed caffeine. I also planned to pay for the bill of the car in line behind me. It was a Friday, and I wanted to have some fun by spreading God's love and anonymously blessing someone else.

As I turned into the parking lot, a couple of other cars hurried to be the next ones in line. They thought they were getting ahead by getting in front of me. I shook my head because I knew that they really would have benefitted from being behind me, because I would have paid for their bill. It made me think of the Bible verse, Matthew 20:16, which says, "So the last will be first, and the first will be last."

Then it dawned on me that it is the same with God and people. He wants to bless us, and He wants the best for us. Unfortunately, though, we don't always believe that He will work things out in the way we want, so we tend to run ahead of Him. We get impatient. We want what we think is the best thing and we want it now. Meanwhile, we miss out on a blessing by not allowing God to lead and by not waiting for Him to work things out.

I know I personally have a bad habit in this area. I often jump and think later. I know I should prayerfully seek God, His plan, and His will first. I should believe that He will work things out. But too often, I don't do it. I see something shiny and I want to grab it.

This fast-paced world we live in plays a big role in why we are this way. We have everything at our fingertips. We don't have to wait until the weekend to go to the bookstore to buy the book we want. Instead, we can download it on our tablet right now. Need something from the store? You don't even have to go there. In many places you can order your groceries online and have them delivered. Drive down any road and you will see someone who is in too big of a hurry. In our small town, my husband and I will sometimes see vehicles pass on sections of road with double yellow lines, and the cars they are passing aren't even going slow. We have too much on our plates, and we need everything on our to-do lists done yesterday. We have too much to do at our jobs and not enough time to do it. We run from work to home with barely enough time to throw dinner on the table before we go to bed and do it all over again the next day.

Part of giving God our whole heart is allowing Him to take the lead in our lives. Often times this means slowing down and waiting for His direction. Psalm 27:14 says, "Wait for the Lord; be strong and take heart and wait for the Lord." The word *wait* can cause many of us to get quite antsy. We don't like to wait for anything. We think that when we are waiting and not actively doing something, it means that we are weak and inadequate. However, when we wait, we are displaying strength and showing the Lord that we want to be obedient to His will.

Of all the pictures of wildlife my husband and I have taken in the mountains, one of my favorites is of a small blue bird just sitting on a fence. I think I like it so much because this bird seems to have it all together. He isn't worried or stressed. He is confident and at peace.

We can be like that too. In fact, there is even a Bible verse about this. Matthew 6:26 says, "Look at the birds of the air; they do not sow or reap or store away in barns, and yet your heavenly Father feeds them. Are you not much more valuable than they?"

We don't have to fall victim to this fast-paced world and its ways. The key is to allow God to lead. It sounds simple, but it's not always easy. It starts with believing that God has our best interests in mind. Then, like the bird on the fence, we can be at peace knowing He is in control. When we know God is in control, we know that He will always bring us His best.

Dying to Self

One step in the process of allowing God to lead, is dying to self. And dying to self is also a vital part of giving God our whole heart. What does "dying to self" mean? It means laying down our own desires and replacing them with what God wants. When we realize that God's ways are better than our ways and that with Him we can have so much more than we could without Him, our wishes will align with His.

In Luke 9:23, Jesus says, "Whoever wants to be my disciple must deny themselves and take up their cross daily and follow me." Let's break this down:

Whoever wants to be my disciple – I hope if you are reading this either you are or you want to be a disciple, or follower, of Jesus. When Jesus said these words, He was seen as a spiritual leader. Many people in His day wanted to follow Him in order to learn and grow. We too should want to learn and grow. But that's not all. The people who Jesus was talking to didn't yet know that He would die for their sins. Since we have this knowledge, that alone should make us want to be followers of Jesus.

Must deny themselves – We must learn to set aside our own desires and wants, in order to align ourselves with God's desires and wants. This might be a painful process and could even cause us much grief. Yet in the long run, the outcome will be beautiful.

And take up their cross daily – Back when Jesus walked the earth, a person who was being executed had to carry their own cross to the place of execution, just as Jesus Himself did. Therefore, I believe in this statement, Jesus is telling us we have die to ourselves, or be willing to die for Him. Note the word *daily*. This means every single day we have to make a conscious decision to lay aside the things that our flesh will want.

And follow me – When we become Christians, we gave our hearts to the Lord. Our number one goal in life should be to follow Jesus. It's not something that is done once, but moment by moment throughout a life-long journey.

When our flesh reads this, it might be tempted to rise up with pride. It might bring to mind all the things we want that we will potentially have to give up. It's true; we might have to give up some things. However, if that's the case, it just means it wasn't good for us and God has a better plan. If God asks us to let something go, then we have to trust that He has our best interests in mind. But we might not necessarily have to give up everything that we want. God cares about our desires and dreams. Psalm 37:4 tells us, "Take delight in the Lord, and he will give you the desires of your heart." We just have to put God first. We have to do everything for Him and His glory.

Every day that we walk this earth, God is molding us. His goal is to make us more like Christ. Scripture says in 1 Thessalonians 4:3, "It is God's will that you should be sanctified." This basically means He wants us to be holy. He doesn't call for us to give some things up out of any meanness, as some may think. He wants what is best for us. He can see our whole story from beginning to end. He knows what will bring the most fruit in our lives. Therefore, dying to self is really based on love, God's love for us and in turn our love for Him. When we approach it from this point of view, it will make it a lot easier on us and we will be more willing to take that step.

The Promised Land

You might be familiar with the story of the spies Joshua and Caleb from the Old Testament. Recall that the Israelites had been slaves in Egypt awaiting the fulfillment of God's promise to bring them into a land of their own. When the time was right, God did deliver them from slavery and bring them out of Egypt. But they had a journey ahead of them with some hurdles to overcome before they could make it to the Promised Land.

In Numbers 13, we read how the Israelites came to the border of the Promised Land and were confronted with its present inhabitants. God told Moses, "Send some men to explore the land of Canaan, which I am giving to the Israelites. From each ancestral tribe send one of its leaders" (v. 2). As instructed, Moses chose twelve men who would go explore the land for forty days. They were told to assess the people who lived there and were also charged with evaluating the land, soil, trees, fruit, and so on.

When they returned to the camp, ten out of twelve men came back with a sense of fear. They felt that the people who lived there were too strong and powerful for the Israelites to defeat. Yet there were two men, Joshua and Caleb, who had faith that they could take possession of the land. Unfortunately, the ten men with a negative attitude spread a bad report among the rest of the Israelites and had them feeling fear as well. We read in Numbers 14:1-4:

> *That night all the members of the community raised their voices and wept aloud. All the Israelites grumbled against Moses and Aaron, and the whole assembly said to them, "If only we had died in Egypt! Or in this wilderness! Why is the Lord bringing us to this land only to let us fall by the sword? Our wives and children will be taken as plunder. Wouldn't it be better for us to go back to Egypt?" And they said to each other, "We should choose a leader and go back to Egypt."*

A little later, in Numbers 14:7-9, Joshua and Caleb tried to talk sense into the people. They said,

> *"The land we passed through and explored is exceedingly good. If the Lord is pleased with us, he will lead us into that land, a land flowing with milk and honey, and will give it to us. Only do not rebel against the Lord. And do not be afraid of the people of the land, because we will devour them. Their protection is gone, but the Lord is with us. Do not be afraid of them."*

These words did not put the Israelites at ease. In fact, they talked about stoning the two men. The Lord was not pleased with the way His people were behaving. He became very angry, and in the end, He did not allow any of the naysayers to enter the new land.

In Numbers 14: 28-35, the Lord spoke to Moses and his brother Aaron:

> "So tell them, 'As surely as I live, declares the Lord, I will do to you the very thing I heard you say: In this wilderness your bodies will fall—every one of you twenty years old or more who was counted in the census and who has grumbled against me. Not one of you will enter the land I swore with uplifted hand to make your home, except Caleb son of Jephunneh and Joshua son of Nun. As for your children that you said would be taken as plunder, I will bring them in to enjoy the land you have rejected. But as for you, your bodies will fall in this wilderness. Your children will be shepherds here for forty years, suffering for your unfaithfulness, until the last of your bodies lies in the wilderness. For forty years— one year for each of the forty days you explored the land—you will suffer for your sins and know what it

is like to have me against you.' I, the Lord, have spoken, and I will surely do these things to this whole wicked community, which has banded together against me. They will meet their end in this wilderness; here they will die."

It should have taken the Israelites eleven days to travel from Egypt to the Promised Land. Instead, it took them forty years. And the adults of this group never did get to inhabit the new land, except for Joshua and Caleb. How sad. This story shows me how important it is to allow God to lead in our lives. The majority of the Israelites weren't willing to believe that God was on their side. They let their obstacles overshadow their God. Only Joshua and Caleb were willing to be obedient to the Lord. They knew God was with them and would help them defeat their enemies. They knew that God had their best interests at heart. They knew that God's ways were better than their ways.

Sometimes God might lead us down a path that doesn't make sense to our human mind. If we want to give God our whole heart, though, it is important to remember that His ways are not our ways. He can see the beginning and the end. And He knows the best path to take. When we allow God to lead in our lives, we will always have success and we will always see victory.

Reflection

Do you find it difficult to allow God to lead in your life?

_____

_____

_____

_____

Are you willing to follow Jesus daily in your life?

_____

_____

_____

_____

Do you believe that God has your best interests in mind?

Chapter 9 – Conclusion

On a recent vacation to the mountains, I counted all the churches I saw along our drive. It started out as a way to pass the time on the long trip, but seeing the churches also brought me comfort. Each church I saw made me smile and think about God's presence. After we arrived at our destination, I kept noticing churches each day of the trip. And when my husband and I arrived home at the end of the week, I still spotted churches wherever we went. They seemed to call to me. They were like a sign of hope, reminding me that God was always there.

Recently, when I was on my way home from work, there was an accident on the interstate, which meant I took some back roads for part of my commute. The only problem was that the back roads were congested as well. It was a Friday, and I just wanted to get home. It was tempting to get aggravated. However, along my drive, since I was going a different route, I happened to notice eight churches. I could have been annoyed, but with the sight of the churches, I just smiled. I felt like God was reminding me He was there, I was safe, and everything was okay.

God is in every little thing. When I see the shape of a heart in the froth of my cappuccino, I see God reminding me of His love. When I see the sunrise peeking over the horizon, I see God wishing me a good morning. When I see the sky streaked with brilliant yellows, oranges, and pinks in the evening, I see God sending me a hug as I end my day. When I am having a bad day and a coworker stops by my desk to talk, I see God sending an angel to make me feel better. When I get to work and back home safely, I see God protecting me. When I see God in everything, I know I am always safe and held in His loving arms.

And I believe this is the reason why I now love the sight of a church. It gives me a feeling of peace during my hectic days, and it reminds me that I am never alone. As Christians, we have the Holy Spirit with us everywhere we go. So we can have a sense of His presence at any given time. God is always there. He is a God of love who wants to have a relationship with you. He longs to be the anchor in your life. He is waiting to be your fulfillment. And He wants you to give Him your whole heart.

Psalm 121 is special to me because it is one of the psalms which my grandmother had memorized. More than that, I believe it is also a beautiful picture of how the Lord watches over us. When you long to feel the love of the Lord, when you wish He could wrap you in a hug, or when you just feel out of sorts, perhaps reading these words will help strengthen your faith and give you peace:

I lift up my eyes to the mountains—
where does my help come from?
My help comes from the Lord,
the Maker of heaven and earth.

He will not let your foot slip—
he who watches over you will not slumber;
indeed, he who watches over Israel
will neither slumber nor sleep.

The Lord watches over you—
the Lord is your shade at your right hand;
the sun will not harm you by day,
nor the moon by night.

The Lord will keep you from all harm—
he will watch over your life;
the Lord will watch over your coming and going

both now and forevermore.

A Prayer to Start Your Day

We will still make mistakes, because we are human. None of us will be perfect. But we can be thankful because in Lamentations 3:22-23 Scripture says, "Because of the Lord's great love we are not consumed, for his compassions never fail. They are new every morning; great is your faithfulness." Moment by moment, we can start fresh. If we see we've made a mistake, we don't have to let it bring us down. That's what the enemy wants; it is not what God wants. Instead, God wants us to press forward with confidence in the knowledge that we belong to the King of kings.

In order to help start my day off on the right foot and keep the proper frame of mind throughout my day, I recite a prayer I wrote each morning. I wanted to share it with you as well. The prayer has four sections that I believe cover almost anything we might face in our day.

Dear heavenly Father,

Today help me to focus on You and give You my whole heart. Whatever I do today, I pray it is part of Your will for my life. Help me to draw closer to You and grow in faith.

I put on the armor of Christ this morning [see Ephesians 6:10-17], for I know that each day may bring new spiritual battles. But I will remember that I can do all things through Christ who strengthens me [see Philippians 4:13]. And You have not given me a Spirit of fear; but of power, love, and self-discipline [see 2 Timothy 1:7].

Search my heart, Lord, and show me areas that are not in alignment with Your will. Help me to remove everything that You do not like. Replace it all with You. Help me to overflow with You, with the anointing, with the fruit of the Spirit, with the Holy Spirit.

Help me to be loving to everyone I encounter. Help me to be a reflection of You. I pray that I am loving toward my family, friends, coworkers, and even strangers. Help me to remember that I might be the only piece of Jesus that those people see today.

In Jesus' holy name I pray,
Amen

What Will You Decide?

One Sunday I sat at a traffic light watching vehicles cross in front of me. One four-door sedan had a middle-aged lady driving it and next to her a small poodle mix that was stretching so he could stick his nose out the window. Perhaps they were out for a leisurely drive. Then there came a small four-door pickup truck pulling a trailer with a lawn mower on it. I assumed the man driving was working that day. A larger green pickup passed by next, with a few tires loaded in the back of the truck. Had this man just come from purchasing new tires? Then a small SUV passed in the opposite direction with an elderly man and woman who appeared to have come from church.

As I sat at the light that day, I thought about all the people who passed by. All those people were going somewhere and they all had a story. I made assumptions based on what I saw. However, the story that I saw on the outside didn't necessarily tell me what was happening on the inside. This is true for every one of us, every single day. On the surface our lives look one way, but often times there is something else brewing underneath. Perhaps on the outside things in our lives look perfect, while on the inside we are dealing with a storm.

Just like all the people I watched driving by in their vehicles, you too have a story. I don't know what it is, and I don't know where you are going. I don't know what your life looks like on the outside. And I don't know what is taking place on the inside. But I do know one thing, and this pertains to everyone. No matter what your story is, no matter what your life looks like on the outside, no matter what is truly occurring on the inside, and no matter where you are headed, when you decide to give the Lord your whole heart, your life will drastically change for the better. You will find true fulfillment in life. You will no longer have to search for happiness, because you will have peace in your heart. You might face storms in life, but you will not be tossed around in the wind, because you will have an Anchor holding you down.

The choices you make today matter. The things you do today affect your future. The little things in your daily life are important. They all add up. As I said at the beginning of this book, some birthdays hit us harder than others. I don't want to wake up on another birthday questioning where the years went. I don't want to ask myself if I made the best choices in life each day. I don't want to wonder what my life would have looked like if only I had given God my whole heart.

And I don't want you to go through that either. When you give God your whole heart, you will have no regrets. Things in your life might not always go the way you would prefer, but you will know that you are anchored to Him. You will know that you are safe. You will have peace, contentment, and true fulfillment. I hope and pray that you will make that decision to give God your whole heart.

Accepting Jesus into Your Life

Do you have a personal relationship with God? If not, then I invite you to begin one today. I promise you that you will not regret it. Having a relationship with God will bring comfort and peace into your life.

Having a relationship with God starts with accepting Jesus. The Bible says that we "all have sinned and fall short of the glory of God" (Romans 3:23). And there is nothing we can do on our own to achieve salvation (Ephesians 2:9).

But the good news is that "If you declare with your mouth, 'Jesus is Lord,' and believe in your heart that God raised him from the dead, you will be saved" (Romans 10:9). This is because Jesus paid the price that we could never pay. He died for all of our sins. He took them on Himself so that we might have eternal life. Then three days after His death, Jesus rose from the dead. This ultimately defeated death and gave us the hope of salvation.

A life with Jesus by your side can be so very freeing. Every day we struggle with the weight of the world on our shoulders. Yet it doesn't have to be that way. We can accept Jesus into our hearts, and let God handle our troubles. If you believe this, I invite you to pray this prayer now:

Lord Jesus, I ask You to please forgive me of my sins. I believe that You died on the cross for me and rose from the grave three days later. I can never thank You enough for paying for my sins. Thank You for hearing my prayer. Thank You for Your unconditional love. I am ready to hand my life over to You. I am ready to walk in Your strength and power. I am ready for You to be the center, purpose, and meaning of my life. I am ready for You to be my Lord and Savior. In Jesus's name I pray. Amen.

If you prayed this prayer, congratulations! I would love to hear from you. Please contact me at bridgetathomas.com/contact.

Acknowledgements

First, I want to thank Jesus. This is all about Him and not about me. Without Him, I am nothing. I thank Him for the gift of salvation and for helping me share it with others.

A huge thank to my husband, Mickey. He has made many sacrifices which have allowed me the time to write this book, and his prayers have kept me going. I love you forever!

Many thanks to my parents and my sisters who have been cheering me on along this entire journey. I love you guys!

Thank you to my cover designer, Stacey. Your encouragement and expertise are truly a blessing to me!

I also want to say thank you to my launch team. These wonderful souls have been there for me with each and every one of my books. I hope you know that your support truly means the world to me.

And a great big thank you to all of my family and friends. So many of you have been an encouragement to me on this journey. There are so many of you that I can't list you all by name. But I want you to know that your support has been such a blessing to me, more than you will ever know.

Thank you to my friend, Lorraine, who has gifted many of my books to her friends. Her love for the Lord, her heart to spread the gospel, and her encouragement have been such a blessing to me.

Thank you to my editor, Brittany. I very much appreciate your guidance and skill.

Thank you to you, the reader! I am grateful that you took the time to read this book. I hope and pray that it has been a blessing to you.

About the Author

Bridget A. Thomas is the author of numerous books that have hit the top of the charts and continue to help many people find true contentment in life. In her spare time, Bridget enjoys reading non-fiction, fiction, and classic literature. She also enjoys crocheting and watching baseball. Bridget and her husband live in Florida, but often travel to the Smoky Mountains in search of black bears and other wildlife. To learn more about Bridget, visit her website, bridgetathomas.com.

One Final Thing

Dear Friend,

Thank you for reading this book! I truly hope you enjoyed it and got some meaning out of it. I really would appreciate your feedback. So would you please take a moment to leave a review on the website where you purchased this book? Thank you so much!

Every Day is a Gift!
Bridget A. Thomas

Made in the USA
Monee, IL
12 November 2019